Views of Europe

Visit the continent at the crossroads of many cultures

ENCYCLOPÆDIA

Britannica®

CHICAGO   LONDON   NEW DELHI   PARIS   SEOUL   SYDNEY   TAIPEI   TOKYO

Views of Europe

I N T R O D U C T I O N

Where is the Emerald Isle? Why was the Berlin Wall built and torn down? What is a fjord? What city in Eastern Europe was called 'Little Paris'?

In *Views of Europe,* you'll discover answers to these questions and many more. Through pictures, articles, and fun facts, you'll learn about the people, traditions, landscapes, and history that make up many of the countries and cities of Europe.

To help you on your journey, we've provided the following signposts in *Views of Europe:*

■ **Subject Tabs**—The coloured box in the upper corner of each right-hand page will quickly tell you the article subject.

■ **Search Lights**—Try these mini-quizzes before and after you read the article and see how much - *and how quickly* - you can learn. You can even make this a game with a reading partner. (Answers are upside down at the bottom of one of the pages.)

■ **Did You Know?**—Check out these fun facts about the article subject. With these surprising 'factoids', you can entertain your friends, impress your teachers, and amaze your parents.

■ **Picture Captions**—Read the captions that go with the photos. They provide useful information about the article subject.

■ **Vocabulary**—New or difficult words are in **bold type**. You'll find them explained in the Glossary at the end of the book.

■ **Learn More!**—Follow these pointers to related articles in the book. These articles are listed in the Table of Contents and appear on the Subject Tabs.

■ **Maps**—You'll find lots of information in this book's many maps.

  ■ The **Country Maps** point out national capitals. **Globes** beside Subject Tabs show where countries are located in the world.

  ■ The **Continent Maps** have a number key showing the location of all countries.

■ The **Icons** on the maps highlight major geographic features and climate. Here's a key to what the map icons mean:

    Deserts and Other Dry Areas   Rainforests

    Polar Regions and Other Frozen Areas   General Forests

    Mountains

Edinburgh Castle sits high up on Castle Rock, some
75 metres above the rest of Edinburgh. The site may
have been used as a fortress as early as the 6th century.

Views of Europe
TABLE OF CONTENTS

INTRODUCTION 3

Europe: Unity in Diversity 6

Western Europe

Portugal: Life on the Iberian Peninsula 8

Spain: A Distinctive European Country. 10

England: Heart of a Language and Culture 12

   London, England: City on the Thames. 14

Scotland: Land of Mountains and Heath 16

Ireland: The Emerald Isle 18

Wales: Land of the Song 20

France: Country of Castles, Wine, and History 22

Brussels, Belgium: Belgium's Beautiful Capital 24

The Netherlands: Country of Windmills and Dykes . . 26

Central Europe

Germany: A Country Reunited 28

Switzerland: Snow and Chocolates. 30

Vienna, Austria: City of Music 32

Czech Republic: New Beginnings in a Historic Land . 34

Poland: Country in the Heart of Europe 36

Northern Europe

Reykjavik, Iceland: Bay of Smokes. 38

Copenhagen, Denmark: City of the Little Mermaid . . 40

Norway: Land of Fjords and Mountains 42

Sweden: Scandinavia's Largest Country. 44

Russia: The Largest Country in the World 46

Eastern and Southern Europe

Bucharest, Romania: 'Little Paris' 48

Sofia, Bulgaria: Bulgarian Capital
of Today and Yesterday. 50

Serbia and Montenegro: A Country of Many
Cultures 52

Ukraine: Borderland Country 54

Greece: Land of Islands. 56

   Athens, Greece: City of the Acropolis. 58

Italy: A Tourist's Delight 60

GLOSSARY 62

INDEX 63

Britannica® LEARNING LIBRARY

Have a great trip!

Which of these rivers can be found in Europe?
a) Rhône
b) Mississippi
c) Nile

Stonehenge, a mysterious ancient monument in southern England.
© Royalty-Free/Corbis

19

31

38

20

47

12

11

32

43

14

13

36

22

24

4

36

33

45

30

16

5

25

23

10

3

40

28

15

44

18

35

41

8

21

6

39

37

29

2

46

26

17

34

42

7

1

27

9

DID YOU KNOW?
Did you know that the automobile was invented in Europe? A German man named Benz came up with the first true petrol-powered car. He named it after his daughter, Mercedes.

Leaning Tower of Pisa, a famous tilting building in Pisa, Italy.
© Royalty-Free/Corbis

Unity in Diversity

Europe is a continent of many countries and many different peoples. Much of it is made up of islands and peninsulas. A peninsula is a piece of land surrounded by water on three sides. Europe's islands include Iceland and the British Isles in the Atlantic Ocean and Corsica, Crete, Malta, and Cyprus in the Mediterranean Sea. Europe's main peninsulas are the Scandinavian, Iberian, Italian, Balkan, and Jutland peninsulas.

Europe also has many mountain ranges. Important ones are the Pyrenees, the Alps, the Apennines, the Carpathians, and the Balkans. Its long rivers include the Volga, the Danube, the Don, the Rhine, the Rhône, and the Oder. These rivers and the **canals** that connect many of them have carried people and products for many, many years.

The rivers also provide water for Europe's farms. Wheat and barley are two of Europe's major crops. Southern Europe specializes in fruits, vegetables, olives, and wines. Other crops include oats, maize, sugar-beets, and potatoes.

Europe is one of the world's major industrial regions. In fact, the **Industrial Revolution** began in Europe. Today the factories of Europe make many products, including electrical goods, motor vehicles, aircraft, and computers.

In the first half of the 20th century, Europe was the centre of two world wars. After World War II, many Eastern European countries had **communist** governments while many in Western Europe had **democratic** governments. By the early 21st century, most Western European countries had joined together to form the European Union (EU). Many EU countries share the same money - called the 'euro'. Most Eastern European countries want to join the EU too.

LEARN MORE! READ THESE ARTICLES...
FRANCE • GERMANY • RUSSIA

COUNTRIES OF EUROPE

1. Albania
2. Andorra
3. Austria
4. Belarus
5. Belgium
6. Bosnia and Herzegovina
7. Bulgaria
8. Croatia
9. Cyprus
10. Czech Republic
11. Denmark
12. England
13. Estonia
14. Finland
15. France
16. Germany
17. Greece
18. Hungary
19. Iceland
20. Ireland
21. Italy
22. Latvia
23. Liechtenstein
24. Lithuania
25. Luxembourg
26. Macedonia
27. Malta
28. Moldova
29. Monaco
30. Netherlands
31. Northern Ireland
32. Norway
33. Poland
34. Portugal
35. Romania
36. Russia (part)
37. San Marino
38. Scotland
39. Serbia and Montenegro
40. Slovakia
41. Slovenia
42. Spain
43. Sweden
44. Switzerland
45. Ukraine
46. Vatican City
47. Wales

Answer: a) Rhône

Life on the Iberian Peninsula

Portugal is a small country in south-western Europe. Its capital is Lisbon, and its only neighbour is Spain. Together, Spain and Portugal make up the Iberian **Peninsula**.

Northern Portugal is quite hilly, with many oak, beech, chestnut, and pine forests. Southern Portugal has mostly **plateaus** and plains. Brush and grasslands cover the plains of the south. Portuguese farmers grow wheat, maize, potatoes, and grapes. And although olives grow wild in Portugal, many farmers also plant their own olive trees. Portugal's many cork oak trees provide much of the world's supply of cork. Portugal is also famous for its many varieties of wine, including port and Madeira.

Summers in Portugal are dry and mild. Many tourists go to Portugal in the summer to see the beautiful museums, castles, and old churches. Others go to tour historic cities, such as Lisbon, Coimbra, and Porto. And many go to enjoy Portugal's many beaches.

The national sport of Portugal is *futebol* (football, or soccer). Portuguese bullfighting is also very popular. It is different from bullfighting in other countries, however. Portuguese bullfighters don't kill the bull in the ring.

Folk music and folk dancing are popular traditions, and most villages have their own *terreiro*, or dance floor. One of the most popular regional dances is the *fandango*. The Portuguese are especially fond of *fado*, a traditional folk song that reflects a sad mood.

Portugal is also famous for its explorers. Ferdinand Magellan led the first expedition to sail around the world, and Vasco da Gama opened up a trade route around Africa to Asia.

Lisbon

LEARN MORE! READ THESE ARTICLES...
FRANCE • ITALY • SPAIN

SEARCH LIGHT

Portugal shares much of its culture with the people of Spain. Why do you think this is true?

Many people travel to Portugal to enjoy the country's beautiful sunny beaches.
© Nik Wheeler/Corbis

Answer: The only country to share a border with Portugal is Spain. So the Portuguese people have had much more contact with the Spanish than any other people.

DID YOU KNOW?

With all the rock stars that have come from the United States and England, you might think that the guitar was invented there. The modern electric guitar was invented in the States, but the guitar itself probably originated in Spain in the early 1500s.

A Distinctive European Country

Spain is a country in the south-western corner of Europe. The capital city is Madrid. Spain borders Portugal and France, but most of the country lies along the Mediterranean Sea and the Atlantic Ocean. The country's beautiful beaches are favourite European holiday spots.

Spain's history is rich and complex. It differs in many ways from other Western European countries. For instance, several Islamic states were formed on its territory, some lasting for centuries. Most other Islamic states lie farther to the east, in the Middle East, or to the south, in North Africa. Modern Spain's cultural variety shows in the different languages spoken there, including Catalan, Basque, Gallego, and, of course, Spanish.

In the 1500s and 1600s, Spain was a world power. It had a powerful navy called the Spanish Armada, and it was the first country to **colonize** much of the Americas. That's why so many people in South America, Central America, Mexico, and the United States speak Spanish and are of Hispanic **heritage**.

Spain features seafood in much of its cooking, with dishes such as paella, a fish-and-rice dish. Spanish farmers are major producers of pork, poultry, beef, and lamb. They also grow wheat, barley, maize, sugar-beets, beans, and olives. Spain also grows grapes for its large wine industry.

Bullfighting has long been a favourite pastime of Spaniards. And football (soccer) is also very popular. Another activity found in Spain is the music and dancing known as *flamenco*. *Flamenco* came to Spain with the Caló (Gitano) people, more commonly known as Gypsies. It is played on guitar as the dancers click wooden castanets and stamp their feet rhythmically.

LEARN MORE! READ THESE ARTICLES...
FRANCE • ITALY • PORTUGAL

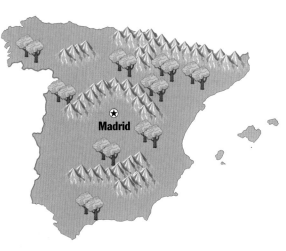

Madrid

This village in Spain overlooks one of the country's many vineyards.
© Patrick Ward/Corbis

Answer: Spain conquered many other areas of the world during its Golden Age in the 1500s and 1600s. Those areas eventually adopted many Spanish customs, as well as the language.

11

The English countryside contains many small villages such as this one in the south-central Cotswold district.
© Nik Wheeler/Corbis

Heart of a Language and Culture

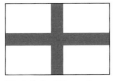 English is one of the world's most widely spoken languages. This is partly because it was the language of the British Empire. The empire once controlled so much of the world that it was said that the Sun never set on the British Empire.

England, the birthplace of English, takes up most of the island of Great Britain. It is one of the four lands that form the United Kingdom. The English that people speak there today is quite different from the English that was spoken long ago. If you were to read a book by Geoffrey Chaucer, one of the early writers of English, someone would have to explain to you what many of the words mean.

England has produced many famous writers since Chaucer. They include such poets as John Milton and Percy Bysshe Shelley, and such novelists as Jane Austen and Charles Dickens. England is also known for its theatre. That art has remained important since the time of the playwright William Shakespeare more than 400 years ago.

England's Oxford and Cambridge are two of the oldest universities in the world. The country's contributions to classical and folk music, as well as to rock-and-roll, are also important. It's hard to imagine what rock would be like without English performers such as the Beatles, the Rolling Stones, and David Bowie.

The English people also invented two of the world's most popular sports: football (known as 'soccer' in the United States) and cricket.

LEARN MORE! READ THESE ARTICLES…
IRELAND • SCOTLAND • WALES

London
⭐

City on the Thames

London is the capital of the United Kingdom. It lies in south-eastern England on the banks of the River Thames. Long ago, the Romans built a city near the mouth of the river. They called it Londinium. That's how London got its name.

Guards parade in front of Buckingham Palace.
© Graham Tim—Corbis/Sygma

Tourists and Londoners alike use London's public transportation system. The red double-decker buses are recognized worldwide. And the city's underground railway - called the 'tube' - has been reliably shuttling passengers throughout London since 1884. The city is full of **monuments,** historic buildings, and other interesting sights. The Tower of London is one of the city's oldest structures. It was built by William the Conqueror as a fortress. It also served as a prison, and its famous prisoners included Sir Walter Raleigh and Elizabeth I, before she became queen. The tower is now a museum that contains England's crown jewels.

Other famous buildings include the Houses of **Parliament** (also called Westminster Palace). This building has 1,100 rooms and over three kilometres of **corridors**. It also has a tower clock called Big Ben, whose huge bell weighs more than 13 tonnes. Nearby is Westminster Abbey, an ancient church where British kings and queens are crowned. Buckingham Palace is the home of the queen of England.

London's British Museum is the oldest museum in the United Kingdom. It has a vast collection of objects from all round the world. It also has one of the world's largest libraries. Another well-known museum is Madame Tussaud's, which has wax statues of famous people.

LEARN MORE! READ THESE ARTICLES...
BRUSSELS, BELGIUM • ENGLAND • WALES

DID YOU KNOW?

On 2-5 September 1666 the worst fire in London's history took place. The Great Fire of London destroyed a large part of the city, including most of the civic buildings, Old St Paul's Cathedral, 87 churches, and about 13,000 houses.

The tower clock known as Big Ben is a famous sight in London. It stands next to the Houses of Parliament along the River Thames.

SEARCH LIGHT

Find and correct the mistake in the following sentence: Britain's kings and queens are crowned in Buckingham Palace.

Answer: Britain's kings and queens are crowned in Westminster Abbey.

SEARCH LIGHT

Fill in the gaps: Although many people visit Scotland to see its castles and _____, the country is best known for its natural _____.

DID YOU KNOW?

Haggis, a national dish of Scotland, isn't for everyone. It's a large round sausage made of the liver, heart, and lungs of a sheep, all chopped and mixed with fat and oatmeal and packed into a sheep's stomach and boiled.

Land of Mountains and Heath

Scotland is a nation famous for its natural beauty. It lies on the northernmost part of the larger of the two main British Isles. Pinewood forests dot the area known as the Highlands. Dwarf willows grow on the highest slopes of the Grampian Mountains just below the snow-covered peaks. But perhaps the most famous of Scotland's plant life is the heather, a kind of **heath**. The word heath is also used to describe the wild wide-open stretches of rough land of Scotland's countryside.

Scotland has been part of the United Kingdom since the 18th century. Its capital is Edinburgh. Scotland's largest city is Glasgow, an industrial centre.

The country has made many cultural contributions to the world. Writer Robert Louis Stevenson wrote the well-loved *Treasure Island* as well as the horror story *Dr. Jekyll and Mr. Hyde*. And poet Robert Burns is claimed by Scots as their national poet.

Many visitors to Scotland go there to see its castles and **abbeys**. Tourists to Scotland enjoy the country's wildlife. Deer, foxes, badgers, and wildcats can be seen in the countryside. Golden eagles, peregrine falcons, and kestrels fly overhead. Almost half the world's gray seals breed off the coast in Scottish waters. And sometimes whales can be seen too.

Many tourists also visit the country's largest lake, Loch Ness. Though its famous Loch Ness monster is probably just a legend, many sightings of the monster have been reported. And the possibility that it may exist continues to fascinate many people.

LEARN MORE! READ THESE ARTICLES...
EUROPE • IRELAND • LONDON, ENGLAND

Edinburgh

A Scottish farmer stands in a pasture with one of his Highland cattle. His knee-length pleated skirt, called a 'kilt', is part of the traditional clothing of men from Scotland.
© Dewitt Jones/Corbis

The Emerald Isle

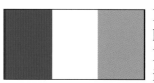

How did Ireland get its nickname of the Emerald Isle?

Ireland is a land with no snakes. Legend has it that St Patrick **banished** them all. But the real reason is that Ireland is an island and snakes have not lived there at least since the last Ice Age, thousands of years ago.

Ireland is the smaller of the two British Isles of north-western Europe. The smaller northern part of Ireland is called Northern Ireland and is part of the United Kingdom of Great Britain and Northern Ireland. Northern Ireland's capital is Belfast. The larger part of Ireland is called the Republic of Ireland, but it is usually simply called Ireland or Eire. Its capital is the city of Dublin.

Because of its location in the Atlantic Ocean, Ireland has a mild **climate** most of the year. It rains quite often, with the hilly parts of the island getting nearly 254 centimetres of rain each year. Much of the land is covered with grass and green moss. Some people describe Ireland as the Emerald Isle because it is so beautifully green. The green lowlands and mild climate make Ireland a good place to rear cattle and sheep. Barley, wheat, and potatoes also grow well. In fact, potatoes were once almost the only food people ate. But in the 1840s, disease ruined the potato crop and many people starved or left Ireland for other countries, especially the United States.

Ireland was once a colony of Great Britain. It gained its independence in the 20th century, although Northern Ireland remains part of the United Kingdom. Ireland is very popular with tourists, and Irish music and culture are famous throughout the world.

LEARN MORE! READ THESE ARTICLES...
LONDON, ENGLAND • SCOTLAND • WALES

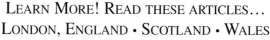

Belfast

Dublin

Cattle graze in a field in County Kerry, Ireland.
© Galen Rowell/Corbis

DID YOU KNOW?
The best-known characters in Irish folklore are fairies called 'leprechauns'. According to legend, they are little old men who live alone and make shoes. They also are supposed to have a hidden pot of gold, which they guard carefully.

Answer: Ireland is such a green and beautiful island that people have for a long time called it the Emerald Isle.

Land of the Song

 Wales is a beautiful land of hills, valleys, and ancient castles. Located on the western edge of the island of Great Britain, it's one of the four countries that today make up the United Kingdom. Wales is called 'Cymru' (pronounced 'Coomrie') in the Welsh language, and its capital, Cardiff, is called 'Caerdydd'. Many people still speak Welsh, but Wales's main language is English.

The rough Welsh countryside was created long ago by rivers of ice called 'glaciers'. Wales's many mountains - including the highest one, Snowdon - were formed mostly from volcanic rock. Along the coast are fabulous cliffs overlooking pebbled and sandy beaches. Seabirds and shorebirds are commonly seen, and bottlenose dolphins live in Cardigan Bay off the west coast.

Coal mining was once the most important part of the Welsh economy. Today, very little coal is still mined in Wales. Many more people now work in manufacturing, especially in the car, chemical, and electronics industries.

Many tourists visit Wales to see its parks and castles and to attend its many music festivals. The largest is the annual Eisteddfod, a celebration of poetry and music that began in 1176. Music is so important in Wales that it is called the 'land of the song'. Choral (group) singing is especially popular amongst the Welsh people.

Nearly 2,000 years ago the ancient Romans built a small fort where the Welsh capital, Cardiff, now stands. Hundreds of years later, invaders from England built a castle on that same site. Cardiff eventually grew there and became an important shipping centre. Cardiff Castle remains one of the city's most impressive buildings.

LEARN MORE! READ THESE ARTICLES...
ENGLAND • IRELAND • SCOTLAND

SEARCH LIGHT

In the Welsh language, the name for the country of Wales is
a) 'Eisteddfod'.
b) 'Caerdydd'.
c) 'Cymru'.

Wales's capital city, Cardiff, had its beginnings in Cardiff Castle. This stone keep, the strongest part of the castle, was built in the 12th century.
© Neil Beer/Corbis

Cardiff

DID YOU KNOW?

Wales's most famous writer was Dylan Thomas, who wrote *A Child's Christmas in Wales*. Roald Dahl, who wrote *Charlie and the Chocolate Factory*, was also born in Wales. So were the actors Richard Burton and Anthony Hopkins.

Answer: c) 'Cymru'.

Country of Castles, Wine, and History

For hundreds of years France was one of the most prized countries of Western Europe. One reason is that France has wonderful farmland. Many types of crops and plants are grown in France because of the plentiful water from France's rivers. And the French have made good use of their generous harvests - fine French cooking has long been internationally appreciated.

Paris

But France may be even better known for its wines. There are miles of lovely green vineyards - areas for growing grapes. The **champagnes** and wines made from these grapes are famous throughout the world.

The French river valleys are full of historic and beautiful old castles, called *chateaux*. These were built of stone, with thick walls that protected the people inside from attacks. At first the *chateaux* were used as forts, but later they were used as homes for the **nobility**. The king and the nobility ruled France until they were overthrown in the French Revolution of 1789. Ten years later the famous leader Napoleon began his rule of France.

Many tourists visit France to see its famous monuments and cathedrals and its beautiful countryside. Some popular spots, such as the palace of Versailles, are located outside the capital city of Paris. Others, such as the Eiffel Tower and the Cathedral of Notre Dame, are inside Paris. Other big French cities include Marseille, Lyon, and Nice.

France is separated from England by a narrow body of water called the English Channel. Today high-speed trains travel between the two countries through the Channel Tunnel, which was built underneath the Channel.

LEARN MORE! READ THESE ARTICLES…
ENGLAND • SPAIN • THE NETHERLANDS

SEARCH LIGHT

Find and correct the mistake in the following sentence: Today high-speed trains travel through the tunnel underneath the English Channel that connects France with Belgium.

Vineyards, where grapes are grown for wine, surround a village in eastern France. French wine is prized all over the world. This village is part of the region that produces wine called Burgundy.

© Michael Busselle/Corbis

DID YOU KNOW?
French writers have won more Nobel Prizes for Literature than writers from any other country.

Answer: Today high-speed trains travel through the tunnel underneath the English Channel that connects France with England.

Belgium's Beautiful Capital

On the banks of Senne River lies Brussels, the capital of Belgium. There is much to see in this historic city known for its lace and chocolate. A more recent feature also sets Belgium apart: together with Strasbourg, France, it's the centre of the European **Parliament**.

One of Brussels' most beautiful old buildings is the Town Hall. It has a tower with the statue of St Michael, the **patron saint** of Brussels. Opposite the Town Hall across the square known as the Grand Place is the King's House. It's now a history museum. On a hill, rising above the modern buildings, is the Church of St Michael and St Gudule. It was built more than 500 years ago.

One of the most popular sights in Brussels is a small bronze fountain in the shape of a naked little boy. He is often called the city's 'oldest citizen' because he has been around since 1619. Other places to visit include the Royal Palace, the Palace of Justice, and the Opera House. There's also the Palace of the Nation, which is the Belgian parliament house.

An unusual and interesting structure in Brussels is the Atomium. It shows how the atoms of a molecule of iron fit together. It is almost 100 metres high and is made of shining metal. It was built for the International Exhibition of Brussels, a fair held in 1958.

Chocolate is not the only kind of food that comes from Brussels. According to some experts, the vegetable called Brussels sprout was first there 800 years ago.

⭐ **Brussels**

LEARN MORE! READ THESE ARTICLES...
FRANCE • GERMANY • THE NETHERLANDS

DID YOU KNOW?
Like many people worldwide, Belgians enjoy fried potatoes (French fries, or chips). But they prefer to eat them with mayonnaise rather than ketchup or some other sauce.

Flowers are sold in Grand Place, a beautiful public square in the city of Brussels. The square began as a marketplace during the Middle Ages.

© Bettmann/Corbis

SEARCH LIGHT

The river that flows past Brussels is called the
a) Seine.
b) Senne.
c) Severn.

Answer: b) Senne.

Country of Windmills and Dykes

The Kingdom of the Netherlands is located in north-western Europe. Although Amsterdam is the country's capital, the Hague is the home of the government and the law courts. Other important cities are Rotterdam and Utrecht. The Netherlands is also known as Holland, and its people are called the Dutch.

Much of the Netherlands is made up of 'reclaimed land'. This means that lakes, marshes, and low-lying land located at or below **sea level** have been drained and made into usable dry land. Such areas are called 'polders'. The polders are surrounded by dams called 'dykes'. Without the dykes, much of the Netherlands would be flooded. People once used windmills to help drain water from flooded lands. Many windmills still dot the landscape. But today electric or **diesel** pumps are used to pump the water out.

Several rivers flow through the centre of the Netherlands. They used to be filled with lobsters and fish, but water pollution has killed many of these animals. Many seabirds and other sea creatures such as **molluscs** can be found in coastal areas.

For a long time, the Netherlands has been known for producing flowers, especially tulips. The butter, cheese, and condensed milk from the country's dairy farms are also famous the world over. Hundreds of years ago, Dutch seamen were the leading merchants of Europe. Today, **commercial** ships still keep the harbours and ports of the Netherlands very busy.

Art has a long tradition in the Netherlands. The most famous Dutch painters are Rembrandt and Vincent van Gogh.

LEARN MORE! READ THESE ARTICLES...
BRUSSELS, BELGIUM • FRANCE • GERMANY

DID YOU KNOW?
Tulips are grown all over the Netherlands, and the country is famous for them.

The many windmills in the Netherlands were once used to drain water from the land.

SEARCH LIGHT

A polder is a
a) windmill.
b) land area that was once under water.
c) machine used to pump water out.

Answer: b) land area that was once under water.

When did Germany become a unified country? (Hint: there is more than one answer!)
a) 1871
b) 1550
c) 1776
d) 1990

DID YOU KNOW?

For German children, the highlight of the Christmas season is St Nicholas Day (6 December). The night before, they leave a shoe outside their bedroom door or by the fireplace. St Nicholas comes during the night to fill the shoes with sweets and gifts.

Houses line a river at Schiltach, a village in the Black Forest region of Germany. The region is named for its thick groves of trees.

© Richard Klune/Corbis

A Country Reunited

Although Germany, in the heart of central Europe, has a long history, it is actually a young country. For many years various princes, dukes, and bishops ruled small states in the region. It was not until 1871 that these became united as a single nation.

Germany has produced many renowned musicians, writers, artists, scientists, and athletes. Such figures include writer Johann Wolfgang von Goethe and composer Ludwig van Beethoven.

In the early 20th century, Germany became involved in two world wars. The country was on the losing side of World War I and as a result suffered through difficult times. Many of the people were unhappy, and some supported Adolf Hitler, who wanted to make Germany strong again. As the leader of the Nazi Party he soon took control of the country. Germany then tried to conquer several neighbouring countries. The conflict over these actions developed into World War II.

After Germany was defeated in 1945, the country was divided into East and West Germany. East Germany became a **communist** country and West Germany became a **democracy**. Berlin, the former capital of Germany, was itself divided in 1961 by the Berlin Wall, built by the East German government. Many families were split up and could no longer visit each other.

In 1989 the Berlin Wall fell and the communist government of East Germany came to an end. On 3 October 1990, Germany became one country again. Berlin became its new, undivided capital.

Berlin

LEARN MORE! READ THESE ARTICLES...
CZECH REPUBLIC • EUROPE • POLAND

DID YOU KNOW?
The Viennese coffeehouse has been a tradition for three centuries. At one time, artists and celebrities gathered at famous literary and theatrical cafés. The word 'café', in fact, comes from a Turkish word meaning 'coffee'.

City of Music

Vienna, the capital of Austria, is famous for its music and its splendid buildings, especially the museums and palaces. What you might find surprising is that Vienna today looks very much like it did hundreds of years ago.

Visitors can take a trip through the city streets in a horse-drawn carriage called a 'fiacre'. No well-dressed fiacre driver would be seen without a colourful shirt and an old-fashioned black hat, according to tradition.

One of Vienna's most impressive sights is the spire of St Stephen's **Cathedral**, which looms over the city. The cathedral bell weighs 20 tonnes. The metal used to make it was melted down from cannons that were captured from the Turkish army in 1711.

Another important building is the State Opera, where many great composers have heard their works performed. That is where the opera composers Richard Wagner and Giuseppe Verdi conducted and where Gustav Mahler was a director. The State Opera opened in 1869 with a performance of Wolfgang Amadeus Mozart's *Don Giovanni*.

Museums have been made from the houses in which the famous **composers** Joseph Haydn, Mozart, Ludwig van Beethoven, Franz Schubert, and Johann Strauss lived and worked. Before they became famous, Haydn and Schubert were members of the Vienna Boys' Choir. The choir was started in 1498 and still performs in the Hofburg Chapel on Sunday mornings. So now you know why Vienna is called one of the music capitals of the world.

Vienna

L EARN M ORE! R EAD THESE ARTICLES...
C ZECH R EPUBLIC • F RANCE • G ERMANY

SEARCH LIGHT

Fill in the gap: Because of the many famous composers who have lived there, Vienna is known as one of the _____ capitals of the world.

One of the many historic buildings in Vienna is the Schonbrunn Palace. The palace was once the home of many Austrian rulers but is now a museum.
© Adam Woolfitt/Corbis

Answer: Because of the many famous composers who have lived there, Vienna is known as one of the music capitals of the world.

33

New Beginnings
in a Historic Land

On 1 January 1993, the nation of Czechoslovakia did a remarkable thing - the former **communist** country split peacefully into two free and independent countries. The eastern section became Slovakia. The western provinces, Bohemia and Moravia, became the Czech Republic. The Czech Republic is the larger of the two new countries. Its capital is Prague.

The Czech Republic has many hills and mountains. These include the Sumava, Ore, Sudeten, and Krkonose mountains. The country is noted for its karst region - a limestone area with many sinkholes, caverns, and underground passages and lakes. Many people visit the Czech Republic especially to participate in winter sports. Others go there for fishing and hunting and to enjoy the beauty of the mountains. Among the country's wildlife, the mouflon, an endangered mountain sheep, is reared in game reserves.

Farming is very important in the Czech Republic. The most important crops are sugar beets, wheat, barley, potatoes, and maize. Northern Bohemia is known for a plant called the 'hop', used in flavouring drinks. The Czech Republic also has many factories that manufacture iron, steel, aluminium, fertilizers, and cement. Cotton, wool, and **synthetic** fibres are also produced and made into clothing.

The Czechs are known for traditional crafts. They make beautiful glass and **porcelain** objects and are especially known for their fine **crystal.** Some people make pretty lace, and others make delightful wood carvings. And among the many Czechs who have contributed to the arts are the novelist Franz Kafka, **composer** Antonin Dvorak, and poster artist Alphonse Mucha. Playwright Vaclav Havel became the first president of the independent Czech Republic.

LEARN MORE! READ THESE ARTICLES…
EUROPE • GERMANY • POLAND

★ **Prague**

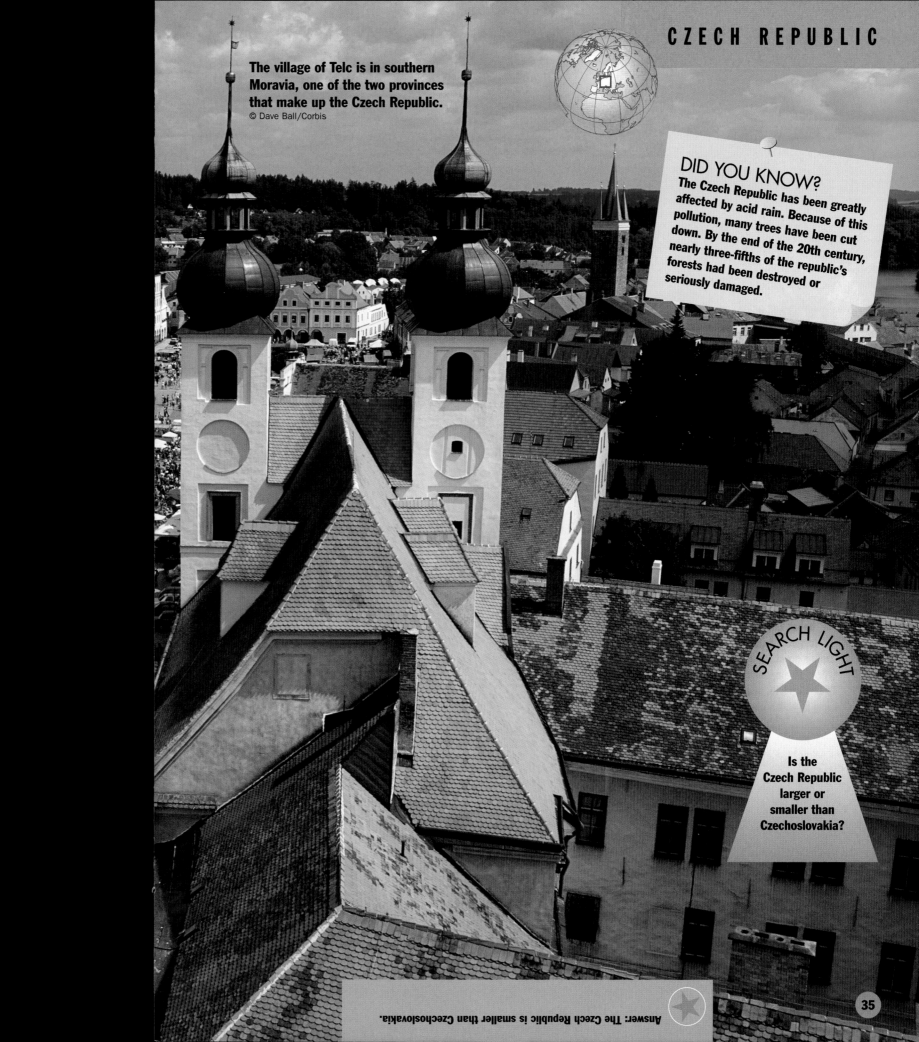

The village of Telc is in southern Moravia, one of the two provinces that make up the Czech Republic.
© Dave Ball/Corbis

DID YOU KNOW?
The Czech Republic has been greatly affected by acid rain. Because of this pollution, many trees have been cut down. By the end of the 20th century, nearly three-fifths of the republic's forests had been destroyed or seriously damaged.

SEARCH LIGHT

Is the Czech Republic larger or smaller than Czechoslovakia?

Answer: The Czech Republic is smaller than Czechoslovakia.

SEARCH LIGHT

Why do you think Poland changed from being Europe's largest state to being no state at all? (Hint: The answer isn't in the article, so you'll have to think about it.)

Country in the Heart of Europe

If people had asked 'Where is Poland?' at different times during the past 1,000 years, they would have been given many different answers.

In the mid-1500s, for example, Poland was the largest country in Europe. But at other times, there was no Polish state at all! In the late 1700s, Poland was no longer a separate country after it had been divided up by the countries of Russia, Prussia, and Austria.

The boundaries of modern Poland were marked out in 1945. Its constitution (laws of government) of 1791 is the oldest in Europe.

About two-thirds of Poland's more than 38 million people live in cities. Warsaw, the capital, is the largest city. Other important cities include Lodz, Gdansk, and Krakow. About 90 per cent of Poles are Roman Catholics. They are especially proud because in 1978 Karol Jozef Wojtyla became Pope John Paul II, the first Polish leader of the Catholic church.

Polish ham is one of the country's most famous exports. In addition to rearing pigs, farmers also rear cattle and sheep throughout the country. Nearly half of Poland's land is used for farming.

Poland has had a changeable history, with shifting boundaries, but it's always enjoyed a rich cultural heritage. In literature Polish poet Czeslaw Milosz won the 1980 Nobel Prize for Literature, and poet Wislawa Szymborska won it in 1996. Frédéric Chopin, a famous composer, was from Poland. And one of the most famous scientists in history, Mikolaj Kopernik, was born in Poland. You may know this great astronomer as Nicolaus Copernicus.

Warsaw

DID YOU KNOW?
During World War II, the Nazis avoided Rozwadow, Poland, because they believed many people there had typhus, a deadly disease. But doctors there had simply injected people with harmless bacteria that looked like typhus in blood tests. This saved many lives.

LEARN MORE! READ THESE ARTICLES...
CZECH REPUBLIC • GERMANY • RUSSIA

The port of Gdansk is one of the largest cities in Poland.
© Bernard and Catherine Desjeux/Corbis

Answer: Poland has been divided and ruled by different countries at various times in its history. The two countries that most recently controlled Poland were Russia and Germany.

37

This power plant produces heat for the city of
Reykjavik by using steam from hot springs.
© Roger Ressmeyer/Corbis

Bay of Smokes

Reykjavik is the capital and largest town of Iceland, a small island country in the North Atlantic Ocean. The word Reykjavik means 'bay of smokes'. The city's name comes from the steaming hot springs nearby. The town is heated by the hot water carried by pipes from these springs. The water is heated by the many volcanoes underneath Iceland.

Even though the city is very far north, it has a fairly mild climate. However, winters are long and very dark. Much of Iceland's area outside the city is covered by **glaciers**.

According to legend, a Viking named Ingolfur Arnarson founded the city about 1,200 years ago. For many years, Reykjavik remained a small fishing village. It was occupied and ruled by the Danes, the people of Denmark. Today Reykjavik is a major fishing port. It is also Iceland's main centre for business. Not surprising for a fishing city, Reykjavik's chief industries are processing fish and building ships.

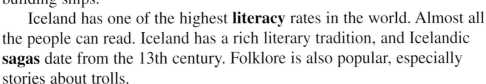

Reykjavik

Iceland has one of the highest **literacy** rates in the world. Almost all the people can read. Iceland has a rich literary tradition, and Icelandic **sagas** date from the 13th century. Folklore is also popular, especially stories about trolls.

The city has many museums and art galleries. The country's traditional cuisine includes many seafood dishes and *skyr*, a dessert made from skimmed milk and served with fresh bilberries.

LEARN MORE! READ THESE ARTICLES...
COPENHAGEN, DENMARK • NORWAY • SWEDEN

DID YOU KNOW?
Apparently it's not uncommon for workers in Iceland to hire a medium to help them if something goes wrong during a construction project. A medium is someone who claims to be able to talk to supernatural creatures.

City of the Little Mermaid

Copenhagen is Denmark's capital and largest city. It is located on two islands: Zealand and Amager. Denmark is an unusual country because it's made up of a peninsula (Jutland) and over 400 islands. What used to be Copenhagen's city centre is located on a little island called Slotsholmen (meaning 'castle **islet**').

In 1167, Bishop Absalon of Roskilde had a fortress built on Slotsholmen. This was the beginning of the city. The Christiansborg Palace replaced the fortress, and now it houses the Danish **parliament** and the Supreme Court. Today the Danish royal family live in the Amalienborg Palace.

To the west of Slotsholmen is the Town Hall. It has a very interesting feature. Apart from the usual offices, it also has Jens Olsen's **astronomical** clock. This huge clock shows the time in different parts of the world. It also shows the **orbits** of the planets and two different calendars.

Nearby is Charlottenborg Palace, the home of the Royal Academy of Fine Arts. The palace was built in the 17th century. Close to it is Tivoli, a world-famous amusement park that opened in 1843.

Copenhagen

If you go farther north, you'll see the Citadel, a military **fortress** still used by the Danish army even though it was built nearly 400 years ago. In the harbour outside the fortress is the statue of the Little Mermaid. It is said to be the symbol of the city. The story of the Little Mermaid is a fairy tale written by Hans Christian Andersen, who spent many years of his life in Copenhagen.

LEARN MORE! READ THESE ARTICLES...
NORWAY • REYKJAVIK, ICELAND • SWEDEN

SEARCH LIGHT

Fill in the gap: The city of Copenhagen lies on two _____.

City natives and visitors alike enjoy the Tivoli Gardens in Copenhagen. Besides its pretty flowers and fountains, Tivoli has restaurants, open-air theatres, and an amusement park with rides and games.
© Steve Raymer/Corbis

DID YOU KNOW?
In World War II, when the Germans occupied Copenhagen, the Danish king rode daily through the city on his horse to give his people courage. When asked why the king had no bodyguard, a boy supposedly said: 'All of Denmark is his bodyguard.'

Answer: The city of Copenhagen lies on two islands.

DID YOU KNOW?
A vast ocean current carries warm water to Norway's coast. This usually keeps the fjords from freezing, even in areas that are north of the Arctic Circle.

SEARCH LIGHT

Fill in the gaps: Two major Norwegian languages are _____ and _____.

Land of Fjords and Mountains

Norway is a country in northern Europe. It lies on the western half of a **peninsula** it shares with Sweden. Together with Denmark, these countries are known as Scandinavia. The many arms of the sea that stretch into Norway are called 'fjords'. The longest and deepest of these is Sogne Fjord. Almost every part of the country is close to the sea or a fjord.

Norway is also covered with mountains. The two highest peaks are Galdhopiggen and Glittertind. Each of them is more than 2,460 metres tall. **Glaciers** can be found in some of the mountain ranges. The Jostedals Glacier is the largest in Europe.

Norway is a leading producer of **oil**, which comes from the North Sea. Many people work in **forestry**, harvesting trees for **timber**. Most of Norway's forests contain evergreen trees, such as pine and spruce. In the south, however, the forests contain ash, birch, and aspen trees. Elk, wild reindeer, lemmings, and wolverines live in the mountains and forests.

Fishing is a major **industry** in coastal areas. Other countries buy fish from Norway, especially frozen cod, canned sardines, and herrings. And whales can be seen too, off the Norwegian coast. Norway's long seafaring tradition includes many famous explorers, such as the Viking explorer Leif Eriksson and the adventurer-scientist Thor Heyerdahl.

Some of Norway's native Sami people (also called Lapps) still practise traditional reindeer herding. Most of the people of Norway speak either Bokmal or Nynorsk, though many also speak English. Painter Edvard Munch, playwright Henrik Ibsen, and composer Edvard Grieg are famous Norwegians who have made important contributions to the arts.

LEARN MORE! READ THESE ARTICLES…
REYKJAVIK, ICELAND · RUSSIA · SWEDEN

Many long narrow arms of the sea called 'fjords' stretch into the western part of Norway. Here a woman looks down on Geiranger Fjord.
© Bo Zaunders/Corbis

Oslo

Scandinavia's Largest Country

 The Kingdom of Sweden in northern Europe is the largest of the Scandinavian countries. **Scandinavia** is the area occupied by Sweden, Norway, and Denmark. Norway and Finland are on Sweden's borders. The rest of the country is bounded by water.

SEARCH LIGHT

As well as fish, what do Swedes get from their rivers that helps them in their everyday lives?

The capital of Sweden is Stockholm, nicknamed the 'Venice of the north'. Like that Italian city, Stockholm has many waterways and bridges. Sweden has many rivers and lakes. And rivers provide half of the country's electric power. The rivers and lakes also contain many varieties of fish.

Sweden is a cold country. But the temperature in each part of the country depends on the **elevation** of the land and how close it is to the sea. The weather is warmer near the sea and colder on the mountains. Evergreen forests of spruce and pine cover more than half of Sweden. In the south there are also deciduous trees (trees that lose their leaves). Because of its rich forests, Sweden is known for its timber, wood **pulp**, paper, and furniture industries.

Within its forests Sweden has many different kinds of animals and birds. There are hares, weasels, shrews, foxes, ermine, and elk. Snipes, plovers, wagtails, partridges, ptarmigans, grouse, and woodcocks are just some of Sweden's many birds.

The Swedes celebrate many special festivals. On December 13 they celebrate St Lucia's Day. On that day young girls wear green wreaths with lighted candles on their heads and serve coffee and buns to older family members. Midsummer's Eve is celebrated with singing and dancing on about June 24, around the time of the longest day of the year.

★ **Stockholm**

LEARN MORE! READ THESE ARTICLES...
COPENHAGEN, DENMARK • NORWAY • RUSSIA

DID YOU KNOW?

Although Sweden can be cold, you may still want to consider moving there when you get older. By law, all Swedish citizens get at least five weeks of paid holiday a year.

Much of Stockholm, the capital of Sweden, is built on islands. The islands are connected to each other and to city districts on the mainland by old bridges and modern overpasses.
© Macduff Everton/Corbis

Answer: Half of Sweden's electricity comes from its rivers. As the rivers flow through large dams, the water turns motors known as 'turbines'. The turbines make electricity.

DID YOU KNOW?
It would take the water from all the rivers in the world a whole year to fill Russia's Lake Baikal just once.

SEARCH LIGHT

Which country has a greater land area than Russia?
a) United States
b) China
c) Romania

The Largest Country in the World

Russia is the largest country in the world - nearly twice the size of China or the United States. In fact, Russia is so large it stretches across two **continents** - Europe and Asia.

Until 1917, Russian **tsars**, such as Peter the Great and Catherine the Great, had long ruled the country. The communist nation known as the Soviet Union was founded in 1922, and Russia was its largest and most important republic. The Soviet Union dissolved in 1991, however, and Russia became an independent country again.

Most of Russia is covered by large rolling plains. Across the plains flow Russia's rivers, including the Volga, the longest river in Europe. 'Mother Volga' flows into the Caspian Sea, the world's largest **inland** body of water. Many of the other rivers drain into the Arctic Ocean or into Lake Baikal, the world's deepest lake. More than one-fifth of all the world's fresh water is in Lake Baikal. That's more water than there is in all five of the Great Lakes in North America put together.

Roughly 145 million people live in Russia. About three-fourths of them live in cities. Moscow, the capital, is the largest city. It has more than 8 million citizens. St Petersburg is the second largest city, with more than 4 million people. Both cities have many world-famous museums and buildings.

Russians have contributed greatly to the arts. The works of writers Aleksandr Pushkin, Leo Tolstoy, and Anton Chekhov are still popular today. So is the music of composer Pyotr Ilich Tchaikovsky. And Russian ballet companies have trained some of the world's most gifted dancers, including Anna Pavlova and Mikhail Baryshnikov.

Moscow

LEARN MORE! READ THESE ARTICLES...
CZECH REPUBLIC • NORWAY • SWEDEN

St Basil's Cathedral is a colourful landmark in Moscow, the capital of Russia.

Answer: No other country is larger than Russia.

Bucharest is the capital and largest city of Romania. It is the centre of business, government, and the arts for the country.
© Sandro Vannini/Corbis

SEARCH LIGHT

Which of these tourist sights cannot be found in Bucharest?
a) Revolution Square
b) Danube River
c) Cretulescu Church
d) Antim Monastery

'Little Paris'

Bucharest, the capital of Romania, has many public squares. A square is an open area that's formed where two or more streets meet. Many of the city's streets and **boulevards** lead into squares. The famous Revolution Square contains the former royal palace and Cretulescu Church, which was built in 1725. It is one of the most beautiful squares in the city. With its tree-lined boulevards and varied **architecture**, Bucharest was once known as 'Little Paris'.

You can experience some of the city's long history in many of its old buildings. The Antim Monastery and the churches of Stavropoleos and Saint Spiridon are treasured for their age and for their fine architecture. The University of Bucharest was founded in 1694.

Bucharest also has preserved much of its history in its many museums. Two of the most popular are the Museum of the History of the City of Bucharest and the National Art Museum, which is now in the royal palace. Some tourists prefer the Village Museum. It is an open-air building near the Arch of Triumph that displays many kinds of peasant houses.

There is much to do in the city, even after the museums close. Bucharest has a national **philharmonic** orchestra, as well as the 'I.L. Caragiale', the National Theatre, which is named after a famous Romanian playwright. There are also a Theatre of Opera and a Ballet of Romania. A typical Romanian meal enjoyed before or after going to the theatre might include a type of cornmeal bread called *mamaliga* with cheese and sour cream.

★ Bucharest

LEARN MORE! READ THESE ARTICLES...
FRANCE • GREECE • SERBIA AND MONTENEGRO

Bulgarian Capital
of Today and Yesterday

Sofia is the capital of the Eastern European country of Bulgaria. It is also the largest city in the country. It lies in a valley in the western part of Bulgaria.

Sofia has had many different names. When the Romans conquered it long, long ago, they called it Serdica. This name came from the Serdi, a tribe of people who had settled there. When it became part of Bulgaria, it was called Sredets. That name means 'in the middle', and it refers to the position of the city in the centre of the Balkan Peninsula. The Turks conquered Bulgaria in the late 1300s. And about that time the city was given the name Sofia, after its St Sofia church. In the Greek language, *sofia* means 'wisdom'.

Like many old cities, Sofia has an old section and a new one. The old section has narrow streets and small houses that are built close to each other. There are many **mosques** in this part of the city. They were built when Bulgaria was ruled by the Turks.

The modern part of the city has large apartment buildings and wide avenues. Most people in Sofia live in these buildings. There are similar apartments and broad roads in the suburbs too.

If you like history, you'd like to visit the churches of St George, Boyana, and St Sofia. You can also see the Alexander Nevsky Cathedral in Sofia. It was built to honour the Russians who helped Bulgaria to become an independent country in the 1870s.

LEARN MORE! READ THESE ARTICLES…
ATHENS, GREECE • BUCHAREST, ROMANIA • SERBIA AND MONTENEGRO

Sofia

DID YOU KNOW?
In Bulgaria, Christmas is celebrated on two days, December 25 and 26. Under communism, religious holidays weren't allowed. So people invented a supposedly 'non-religious' holiday, and they celebrated it the day after Christmas.

Sofia is a busy but beautiful city. Its buildings display a mixture of many different styles of architecture.
© Sandro Vannini/Corbis

SEARCH LIGHT

Choose the answer that puts the city's different names in order from earliest to most recent.
a) Sredets, Sofia, and Serdica
b) Serdica, Sofia, and Sredets
c) Serdica, Sredets, and Sofia

Answer: c) Serdica, Sredets, and Sofia

A Country of Many Cultures

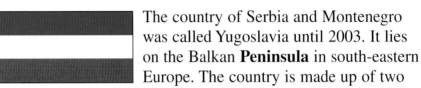

The country of Serbia and Montenegro was called Yugoslavia until 2003. It lies on the Balkan **Peninsula** in south-eastern Europe. The country is made up of two republics. One is Serbia, of which the capital is Belgrade. The other is Montenegro, of which the capital is Podgorica. Until the 1990s Yugoslavia included several other regions that are now independent countries. These were Croatia, Slovenia, Macedonia, and Bosnia and Herzegovina.

Before the 20th century, the country was ruled by many different powers. This made it a country with many **diverse** cultures. The Slavs, the Turks, the Italians, and the Austrians have all influenced the food, folk costumes, and buildings of the country. This large mix of people has sometimes caused problems. In the 1990s there was a war between the Serbs, the Croats, and the Bosnians, and there were many wars earlier in the 20th century. By the beginning of the 21st century, much of the fighting had ended, and the country was beginning to rebuild itself.

The many mountains of Serbia and Montenegro include the Balkan Mountains and the Dinaric Alps. Daravica, at more than 2,400 metres, is the country's highest peak. People raise sheep and goats in the mountain pastures. The main flatland area in the country is the Mid-Danube Plain. It is the most fertile region for growing crops. The main crops are maize, sugar beets, and wheat. Fruits and vegetables are also grown.

Many people go to Serbia to see its very old churches and visit its mineral springs. Montenegro's seacoast, with its beautiful landscape and old stone houses, is also popular.

LEARN MORE! READ THESE ARTICLES…
BUCHAREST, ROMANIA • GREECE • SOFIA, BULGARIA

DID YOU KNOW?

The country was a founding member of the World Chess Federation in 1924. Today, 161 countries belong to the federation, and it is one of the most widespread sports organisations in the world.

Mountains rise up sharply from the coast of Serbia and Montenegro.
© Otto Lang/Corbis

SEARCH LIGHT

Serbia and Montenegro was called Yugoslavia before it took its current name. When did it change its name?

Answer: 2003

Borderland Country

Ukraine has one of the largest populations of any European country. It is located at the eastern edge of Europe, near Asia (the word Ukraine means 'borderland' or 'bordering country'). Ukraine's capital is Kiev, an ancient city that was founded more than 1,000 years ago.

Ukraine is a rather flat country, with only a few mountains. Its major mountains are the Carpathians in the west and the Crimean Mountains in the south. It also contains a portion of the Polissya (also known as the Pripet Marshes), the largest swamp in Europe. The **marshes** have a great variety of wildlife, including elk, wolves, lynx, mouflon (wild sheep), and wild boars.

Ukraine has a rich tradition of oral literature, complete with heroic stories and songs that remain popular today. Ukraine's folk traditions can be seen in the country's many festivals. At the festivals people in brightly coloured folk costumes perform traditional dances and music. The country's written language is similar to Russian and uses the **Cyrillic** alphabet.

The region that is now Ukraine has a long history. Many years ago Kiev was the centre of a country called Kievan Rus. In the 1700s Ukraine came under the control of the Russian **tsars**. In the 19th century it was the main site for battles in the Crimean War between Russia and the Ottoman Turks. Ukraine became part of the Soviet Union in the early 20th century. It was known as the country's breadbasket because it produced large amounts of grain (particularly wheat). In 1991, with the fall of the Soviet Union, Ukraine became an independent country.

LEARN MORE! READ THESE ARTICLES…
RUSSIA • SERBIA AND MONTENEGRO • SOFIA, BULGARIA

SEARCH LIGHT

Ukraine was the centre of what war in the 19th century between Russia and the Ottoman Empire?

Ukrainian folk dancers perform in traditional costumes.
© David Cumming; Eye Ubiquitous/Corbis

DID YOU KNOW?
Even today doctors take the oath of Hippocrates, a famous early Greek doctor. They promise to do no harm and to follow the highest standards in their work.

SEARCH LIGHT

Fill in the gap: Greece includes about _____ islands, though not all have people living on them.
a) 3,000
b) 9,750
c) 2,000

Land of Islands

The country of Greece is surrounded on three sides by seas. To the south is the Mediterranean Sea, to the west is the Ionian Sea, and to the east is the Aegean Sea. More than 2,000 islands in the Ionian and Aegean seas belong to Greece, but people live on only about 170 of them. The islands are divided into two groups - the Ionian Islands and the Aegean Islands - depending on which sea they're in.

As well as its many islands, Greece also has many mountains. The tallest is Mount Olympus. It is 2,917 metres high. Zeus, Ares, Athena, and all the other Greek gods and goddesses were said to live on Mount Olympus.

Greece was the ancient birthplace of Western civilization. The Greeks learned to read and write more than 3,000 years ago. And it was in Greece that the Olympic Games began about 3,500 years ago. The first modern Olympic Games were held in Athens in 1896.

Many great thinkers and philosophers, such as Socrates, Plato, and Aristotle, came from ancient Greece. The country also produced such poets and playwrights as Homer and Sophocles, as well as famous historians such as Herodotus and Thucydides. Pythagoras was one of the earliest mathematicians, and Hippocrates is considered the father of modern Western medicine. Greece was also known for its famous speakers, called 'orators'. One of the most famous was Demosthenes.

Many rare plants grow in Greece, and medicines are made from some of them. But probably the most important plants are the olive trees of Greece. Much of the olive oil bought by people all round the world comes from Greece.

Athens

LEARN MORE! READ THESE ARTICLES...
ATHENS, GREECE • EUROPE • ITALY

Whitewashed houses line the hillside of the island of Santorini in Greece.
© ML Sinibaldi/Corbis

The Theatre of Dionysus in Athens is more than 2,300 years old. If you had lived in ancient Athens, you'd probably have gone to see plays in this huge stone theatre. The whole community was expected to attend performances there.
© Michael Nicholson/Corbis

DID YOU KNOW?
So many tourists visit the Acropolis every year that buses are no longer allowed to drive to the top. The exhaust from the buses was polluting the buildings and causing them to fall apart.

City of the Acropolis

SEARCH LIGHT

How did the first public buildings of modern Athens show the Greeks' respect for the past?

One of the first things you notice in Athens, the capital of Greece, is a flat-topped mass of rock at the city's centre. It's called the Acropolis and is more than 162 metres high. At the top are buildings that were built very long ago. One of them, the famous Parthenon, was built in honour of the goddess Athena. The city was named after her.

Not too far away is the Theatre of Dionysus. This was the city's drama centre. It had 13,000 seats arranged in 67 rows. Nearby is the Odeum theatre, which seated 5,000 people. It is now used for the Athens summer festival of music and drama.

Theatre was very important to the ancient Greeks. When these theatres were built thousands of years ago, the actors wore masks when they performed. The types of plays they performed are called classical Greek tragedies and comedies. These are still performed today.

The modern city grew from the small town at the base of the Acropolis. Many newer parts of the city have been built in the last hundred years or so. Some public buildings were made of white marble to match the buildings on the Acropolis. Today Constitution Square is the centre of the city. And the Old Royal Palace that stands on one side of it is the home of the Greek **parliament**.

When the Olympic Games were revived in 1896, the first Games were held in Athens in the newly remodelled 70,000-seat Panathenaic Stadium. It was originally built in 329 BC for the Panathenea athletic contests, part of ancient Athens' most important festival.

LEARN MORE! READ THESE ARTICLES…
GREECE • ITALY • SOFIA, BULGARIA

Answer: They were made of white marble to match the ancient buildings of the Acropolis.

59

SEARCH LIGHT

Which of the
following can
all be found
in Italy?
a) Milan, Sicily, Rome,
   and Mount Everest
b) Mount Vesuvius,
   Paris, and the
   Statue of Liberty
c) Mount Etna, Pisa,
   and the Alps

A Tourist's Delight

The country of Italy in south-central Europe has a rich history and many interesting places to visit. Rome, Italy's capital, is one of the world's oldest cities. Other historic Italian cities are Milan, Naples, Florence, and Venice, which has many canals.

In Rome the Colosseum is an **arena** where many years ago thousands of people went to watch **gladiators** fight. Vatican City lies within Rome too. It's the world headquarters (seat) of the Roman Catholic church and is where the pope lives. The Sistine **Chapel** in the Vatican is one of the most beautiful buildings in Europe. The ceiling and walls have famous paintings by the famous artist Michelangelo.

Pisa in central Italy is best known for its leaning tower. Soon after its construction started, the ground underneath sank. The Leaning Tower of Pisa leans over so much that to climb its stairs you have to lean in the opposite direction. Engineers have stopped it from sinking. They could have straightened out the whole tower, but then it wouldn't be such fun to visit.

On the island of Sicily in southern Italy is Mount Etna, an active volcano. A thin column of smoke always rises from it, and sometimes red-hot lava spills out. Perhaps even more famous are the breathtaking snow-covered Italian Alps in northern Italy. These mountains aren't volcanoes, though. People travel from all over the world to enjoy winter sports in the Alps.

Italy's wine, food, arts, and culture are prized around the world. Famous Italians include artist Leonardo da Vinci, writers Dante and Petrarch, scientist Galileo, and filmmaker Federico Fellini.

Rome

LEARN MORE! READ THESE ARTICLES...
FRANCE • GREECE • PORTUGAL

G L O S S A R Y

abbey place where a community of monks or nuns live and work; also, the church serving that community

altitude the distance of an object above a specific level (such as sea level) on a planet or other heavenly body

architecture the art of designing and building structures, especially buildings that can be lived and worked in

arena enclosed area used for public entertainment

astronomy (adjective: astronomical) the science of the heavenly bodies and of their sizes, motions, and composition

banish to force or drive away

boulevard wide avenue often having grass strips with trees along its centre or sides

canal artificial waterway for boats or for draining or supplying water to land

cathedral large Christian church where a bishop is in charge

champagne a sparkling white wine

chapel small, sometimes private place for prayer or special religious services

climate average weather in a particular area

colony (plural: colonies; adjective: colonial; verb: colonize) 1) in general, a settlement established in a distant territory and controlled by a more powerful and expanding nation; 2) in biology, a group of similar organisms that live together in a particular place

commerce (adjective: commercial) the buying and selling of goods, especially on a large scale and between different places

communism (adjective: communist) system of government in which all property is owned by the state or community and all citizens are supposed to have a share in the total wealth

composer person who writes music

continent one of the largest of Earth's landmasses

corridor passageway into which compartments or rooms open

crystal clear colourless glass of very good quality

Cyrillic having to do with the alphabet for writing in Russian and other eastern European languages

democracy (adjective: democratic) government in which the highest power is held by the citizens; they either use their power directly (usually by voting) or choose others to act for them

diesel type of fuel-fed engine

diverse varied; different

elevation the height of an object above sea level

forestry the science and work of caring for forests

fortress well-defended place

glacier large river-like body of ice spreading slowly over a land surface

gladiator in ancient Rome, a person who fought to the death as part of a public entertainment

heath low evergreen shrub with needle-like leaves and clusters of small flowers

heritage background or descent

Industrial Revolution period beginning in the 18th century in which the invention of machines changed forever the way people live and work

industry business and manufacturing

inland part of a country away from the coast

islet small island

literacy the ability to read and write

marsh area of soft wet land usually overgrown by grasses and sedges

mollusc any member of a group of animals that have no backbone and are usually enclosed in a shell (for example, snails, clams, or squids)

monument stone or building set up in memory of a person or event

mosque Muslim place of worship

nobility a nation's upper-class social group

oil (or crude oil) liquid taken from the ground and not yet cleaned or separated into such products as petrol and paraffin; also called petroleum

orbit (verb) to travel around an object; (noun) an object's path around another object

parliament the law-making body of some governments

patron saint holy person whose spirit is believed to specially protect a group or place

peninsula a finger of land with water on three sides

philharmonic large orchestra that plays classical music

plateau wide land area with a fairly level surface raised sharply above the land next to it on at least one side

porcelain hard white substance made of clay mixed with other materials; used especially for dishes

pulp 1) in plants, the juicy fleshy part of a soft fruit; 2) in industry, a mashed-up pasty glop such as the plant material used in making paper

resort fancy vacation spot

saga tale of historic or legendary figures and events of Norway and Iceland

Scandinavia area in northern Europe that includes the countries of Denmark, Norway, and Sweden

sea level height of the surface of the sea

synthetic produced artificially

timber wood used for building or carpentry

tsar one of the emperors of Russia until 1917

INDEX

acid rain (pollution)
Did you know? *page* **35**

Acropolis (citadel in Athens, Greece)
Athens *page* **59**

Alps (mountains in Europe)
Italy *page* **61**
Switzerland *page* **30**, photograph
page **31**

Athens (city in Greece) *page* **59**
LEARN MORE *look under* Greece

Austria (country): *look under* Vienna

Baikal, Lake (lake in Russia)
Russia *page* **47**

Belgium (country): *look under* Brussels

Berlin Wall
Germany *page* **29**

Big Ben (clock tower in London,
England, U.K.)
London *page* **14**, photograph *page* **15**

Black Forest (region in Germany)
Germany photograph *page* **28**

Brussels, *also called* Brussel, *or*
Bruxelles (city in Belgium) *page* **24**

Brussels sprouts (vegetables)
Brussels *page* **24**

Bucharest (city in Romania) *page* **49**

Bulgaria (country): *look under* Sofia

bullfighting, *also called* tauromaquia
Portugal *page* **8**
Spain *page* **11**

Central Europe: *look under* Czech
Republic; Germany; Poland;
Switzerland; Vienna

chateaux (French castles)
France *page* **22**

Chernobyl (city in Ukraine)
Did you know? *page* **55**

chess (game)
Did you know? *page* **52**

Christmas (holiday)
Did you know? *page* **28**, *page* **51**

Copenhagen (city in Denmark) *page* **40**

Cymru (country in the U.K.): *look
under* Wales

Czech Republic (country) *page* **34**

Czechoslovakia (historic nation)
Czech Republic *page* **34**

Denmark (country): *look under*
Copenhagen

'Dracula' (book by Stoker)
Did you know? *page* **48**

dykes (dams)
Netherlands, the *page* **26**

Eastern Europe: *look under* Bucharest;
Russia; Serbia and Montenegro; Sofia;
Ukraine

Eisteddfod (Welsh festival)
Wales *page* **20**
LEARN MORE *look under* folk music

England (country in the U.K.) *page* **13**
LEARN MORE *look under* English
Channel; London; Northern Ireland;
Scotland; Stonehenge; Wales

English Channel, *also called* La
Manche (waterway)
France *page* **22**

English language
England *page* **13**

Europe (continent) **10**
LEARN MORE *look under* Athens;
Brussels; Bucharest; Czech Republic;
England; France; Germany; Greece;
Ireland; Italy; Netherlands, the;
Norway; Poland; Portugal; Reykjavik;
Russia; Scotland; Serbia and
Montenegro; Sofia; Spain; Sweden;
Switzerland; Ukraine; Vienna; Wales

European Union (international
organization)
Europe *page* **7**

fishing
Norway *page* **43**

fjords
Norway *page* **43**, photograph *page* **42**

flamenco (music and dance)
Spain *page* **11**

Florence (city in Italy)
Italy photograph *page* **60**

folk dances
Portugal *page* **8**
Ukraine photograph *page* **55**

folk music
Portugal *page* **8**
Wales *page* **20**

food: *look under* Brussels sprouts;
grapes; haggis; olives; potatoes

football, *also called* soccer (sport)
England *page* **13**
Portugal *page* **8**

France (country) *page* **22**

Gama, Vasco da (Portuguese explorer)
Portugal *page* **8**

Germany (country) *page* **29**

glaciers (ice formations)
Norway *page* **43**

Gotthard Tunnel (tunnel in
Switzerland)
Did you know? *page* **31**

grapes (fruit)
France *page* **22**, photograph *page* **23**
Switzerland *page* **30**

Great Britain (country): *look under*
England; Northern Ireland; Scotland;
Wales

Great Fire of London (English
history)
Did you know? *page* **14**

Greece (country) *page* **57**
LEARN MORE *look under* Athens

guitars (musical instruments)
Did you know? *page* **10**

haggis (food)
Did you know? *page* **16**

heath (plant and landform)
Scotland *page* **17**

Hippocratic oath (ethical code)
Did you know? *page* **56**

Hitler, Adolf (German ruler)
Germany *page* **29**

Holland (country): *look under*
Netherlands, the

Iceland (country): *look under* Reykjavik

Ireland (country) *page* **18**

Islam (religion)
Spain *page* **11**

Italy (country) *page* **61**

Kiev (city in Ukraine)
Ukraine *page* **54**

kilt (Scottish clothing)
Scotland photograph *page* **16**

lakes: *look under* Baikal, Lake; Loch Ness

Leaning Tower of Pisa (tower in Pisa, Italy)
Europe photograph *page* **6**
Italy *page* **61**

leprechauns (Irish folklore)
Did you know? *page* **19**

Little Mermaid (statue)
Copenhagen *page* **40**

Loch Ness (lake in Scotland)
Scotland *page* **17**

London (city in England, U.K.)
page **14**

Magellan, Ferdinand (Portuguese explorer)
Portugal *page* **8**

Manche, La (waterway): *look under* English Channel

Matterhorn (mountain in Europe)
Switzerland photograph *page* **31**

medicine (science)
Did you know? *page* **56**

Montenegro (republic): *look under* Serbia and Montenegro

Moscow (city in Russia)
Russia *page* **47**, photograph *page* **47**

Ness, Loch (lake in Scotland, U.K.): *look under* Loch Ness

Netherlands, the, *also called* Holland (country) *page* **26**

Northern Europe: *look under* Copenhagen; Norway; Reykjavik; Russia; Sweden

Northern Ireland (country)
Ireland *page* **18**, flag *page* **18**

Norway (country) *page* **43**

olives
Greece *page* **57**

Olympic Games

Athens *page* **59**
Greece *page* **57**

Paris (city in France)
France photograph *page* **22**

Parliament, Houses of (buildings in London, England, U.K.)
London *page* **14**

Poland (country) *page* **37**

polders (reclaimed land)
Netherlands, the *page* **26**

pollution: *look under* acid rain

Portugal (country) *page* **8**

potatoes (vegetables)
Did you know? *page* **24**
Ireland *page* **18**

Reykjavik (city in Iceland) *page* **39**

Romania (country): *look under* Bucharest

Rome (city in Italy)
Italy *page* **61**, photograph *page* **61**

Russia (country) *page* **47**
LEARN MORE *look under* Ukraine

Scandinavia (region in Europe): *look under* Copenhagen; Norway; Reykjavik; Sweden

Scotland (country in the U.K.) *page* **17**
LEARN MORE *look under* England; Northern Ireland; Wales

Serbia and Montenegro (country) *page* **52**

Serdica (city in Bulgaria): *look under* Sofia

soccer (sport): *look under* football

Sofia (city in Bulgaria) *page* **50**

Southern Europe: *look under* Athens; Greece; Italy; Portugal; Serbia and Montenegro; Spain

Soviet Union (historic nation): *look under* Union of Soviet Socialist Republics

Spain (country) *page* **11**

sports: *look under* bullfighting; football; Olympic Games

Sredets (city in Bulgaria): *look under* Sofia

Stockholm (city in Sweden)
Sweden *page* **44**, photograph *page* **45**

Stonehenge (monument in England, U.K.)
Europe photograph *page* **6**

Sweden (country) *page* **44**

Switzerland (country) *page* **30**

thermal power
Reykjavik photograph *page* **38**

Tower of London (building in London, England, U.K.)
London *page* **14**

tulips (plants)
Did you know? *page* **26**

Ukraine (country) *page* **54**
LEARN MORE *look under* Russia

Union of Soviet Socialist Republics (historic nation)
Russia *page* **47**
Ukraine *page* **54**

United Kingdom (island country): *look under* England; English Channel; London; Northern Ireland; Scotland; Stonehenge; Wales

U.S.S.R. (historic nation): *look under* Union of Soviet Socialist Republics

Vatican City (city and state)
Italy *page* **61**

Vienna (city in Austria) *page* **33**

vineyards
France photograph *page* **23**

Volga River (river in Russia)
Russia *page* **47**

Wales (country in the U.K.) *page* **20**
LEARN MORE *look under* England; Northern Ireland; Scotland

Western Europe: *look under* Brussels; England; France; Ireland; Netherlands, the; Portugal; Scotland; Spain; Wales

windmills
Netherlands, the *page* **26**, photograph *page* **27**

wines
France *page* **22**

World War II
Did you know? *page* **37**, *page* **41**
Germany *page* **29**

Yugoslavia (historic nation)
Serbia and Montenegro *page* **52**